PRAISE FOR THE ULTIMATE CAREGIVER

The Ultimate Caregiver is a contemplative book… a book of stories, prayer, and practical steps for care givers and care-receivers as they are on the meditative path toward wholeness.

In a time when we are not often encouraged to be authentic, this book is a breath of fresh air… filled with pages of understanding and acceptance of all our feelings and how they serve us in moving toward wholeness.

In this beautiful, sensitive way of speaking to all who struggle through life's challenges, the book heightens our awareness of the tight thread that binds us all, caregivers and care-receivers alike, to the Ultimate Caregiver. It is beautifully written... full of insight and wisdom... a gift to all who read it.

Julane Borth
Co-Founder, Spiritual Director
EWF International
Oklahoma City, OK

THE ULTIMATE
CAREGIVER

THE ULTIMATE
CAREGIVER

*Words from the Cross to
the Caregiver's Heart*

WRITTEN BY
BOB WILLIS

Tate Publishing & Enterprises

Published by Tate Publishing & Enterprises, LLC
127 E. Trade Center Terrace | Mustang, Oklahoma 73064 USA
1.888.361.9473 | www.tatepublishing.com

Tate Publishing is committed to excellence in the publishing industry. The company reflects the philosophy established by the founders, based on Psalm 68:11,
"The Lord gave the word and great was the company of those who published it."

Book design copyright © 2008 by Tate Publishing, LLC. All rights reserved.
Cover design by Lindsay B. Behrens
Interior design by Joey Garrett

Published in the United States of America

ISBN: 978-1-60696-256-5
1. Care Giving, Christian Living
2. Grief, Aging, Journaling
00.00.00

The Ultimate Caregiver
is dedicated to:
caregivers who in reality are
"Care-Grievers"
and their loved ones, the care-receivers

ACKNOWLEDGMENTS

First, I want to give thanks to my Lord and Savior, Jesus Christ, for His salvation, His blessings, and His calling upon my heart to work with grief and grievers. I am grateful He reveals Himself as the Ultimate Caregiver.

I especially want to give thanks to my wife, Lynn, for her love, patience, understanding, and support. She was my number one cheerleader during the process of putting this book together. Lynn understood and accepted my need to write in the middle of the night, or in the early hours of the morning.

Also, I want to thank Donna Golden Boyd for sharing her God-given gift of poetry to enhance the content and heart of this book. The majority of the poems included in this book were written by Donna while serving as the caregiver for her husband, Howard.

My appreciation is also extended to Lisa Boone, Ruth Ann Frick, and Phyllis Rogers, for their review and input into the manuscript during the development stage.

A special thank you goes to the Hospice of Oklahoma County staff, patients, family members, volunteers, and caregivers for their lessons in living life to the fullest.

Finally, I wish to acknowledge the participants of grief support groups over the years for sharing their broken hearts, their tears, their grief, their mourning, and their courage.

Blessings,
Bob Willis

TABLE OF CONTENTS

INTRODUCTION

Christ spoke to us from His death bed. The words He spoke over 2000 years ago are very significant and applicable to modern day caregivers and their loved ones, the care-receivers. Suspended on a cross between sinful earth and sinless heaven, He took on the role as the Ultimate Caregiver for all mankind. The words He spoke from the cross relate to forgiveness, faith, providing for family, abandonment, the agony of suffering, the completion of a life purpose, and placing total trust in His heavenly Father. These are pertinent issues for caregivers and their loved ones.

The One familiar with grief, "a man of sorrows" (Isaiah 53:3), was hanging on the cross. Huddled at the foot of the cross were His family and friends, each one experiencing the gut wrenching agony of their own grief. In the midst of their confusion and their pain, they were lovingly gathered at the feet of the Ultimate Caregiver.

There are several subjects addressed within the pages of this book. Material is presented to provide spiritual and emotional support for caregivers and care-receivers. Grief is being experienced by everyone involved in a life crisis, so there are elements in each chapter to guide the expression of feelings.

Recently I was involved with the SomeOne Cares Conference in Ridgecrest, North Carolina. This conference was designed to provide support, education, and guidance to Christian caregivers and church leadership. I was to lead my first session at nine on Friday morning, but God got my attention much earlier than that. At 1:57 on that Friday morning I awoke suddenly. I did not hear God's voice, but I felt God's voice. He impressed upon me that although I thought I was there to speak to caregivers, they were actually more than caregivers. It was during that early morning hour that God provided a new term to me. He revealed to me that I was there to speak to care-grievers. Care-grievers! Caregivers are grieving changes each moment while providing care to their loved one. The Ultimate Caregiver for all of mankind reminded me that grief is an integral part of providing care for our loved ones.

Each circumstance will be different. Some turning the pages of this book will be providing care for a loved one, and others will be on the receiving end of that care. The Ultimate Caregiver is reaching for your heart. Specific attention is given to the needs of the caregiver as they pour their heart into their work. Care-receivers are also given the opportunity to communicate feelings as they walk this difficult journey with the Ultimate Caregiver.

Bob Willis

> There are only four kinds of people in this world. Those who have been caregivers, those who are currently caregivers, those who will be caregivers, and those who will need caregivers.
>
> Rosalyn Carter

A VITAL TRUTH

There is a significant truth that needs to be stated at the beginning of this book. Without this basic understanding, the content of the book will not be clear or accepted.

The vital truth: we grieve the loss of anything valuable to us; we grieve the loss of normalcy; we grieve change.

It is easy to have the mindset that grief only follows a death. Society would love for everyone to accept that myth because we live in a grief defying society. Since grief is the normal and natural response to a loss, let's consider some of the grief issues facing caregivers and their loved ones, the care-receivers. Here is a list of some areas we may grieve when we experience changes. Can you relate to a feeling of loss in any of these areas?

- Loss of health
- Loss of dreams
- Loss of control
- Loss of intimacy
- Loss of support
- Loss of security
- Loss of inner peace
- Loss of plans
- Loss of laughter
- Loss of energy
- Loss of tomorrow
- Loss of faith
- Loss of routine
- Loss of normalcy

Caregivers, and their care-receivers, are faced with constant changes. A change in any of the areas listed above can produce some very normal grief responses. Some of these normal responses to change may be:

fatigue; feeling cheated, overwhelmed with added responsibilities, abandoned, or numb; experiencing mood swings, feelings of guilt, regret, loss of concentration; anger, fear of the unknown, anxiety, and tears at unexpected times. A list of normal responses to change is provided in Appendix A.

We can actually grieve the loss of what could have been, what should have been, even what might have been. The loss of our dreams and our plans are very real losses. It is very normal to feel robbed and cheated when circumstances change our life plans. One purpose of this book is to provide healthy outlets for expressing these feelings of grief.

It is impossible to see another person's grief. Grief is personal and private for each person. No one grieves in the same manner, even if they are part of the same family experiencing the same changes. We grieve according to our personality, the closeness of our relationships, and other losses in our life. There are no cookie cutter grievers. The ways we react to changes and respond to losses in life are as unique as our fingerprints.

When feelings of grief are expressed openly, they become mourning. A good definition of mourning is grief gone public. When we see someone's tears, we do not see their grief, but we are observing the outward expression of the inward pain. We are seeing them mourn.

Jesus did not say, "Blessed are those who grieve, for they shall be comforted." He did say, "Blessed are those who mourn, for they shall be comforted" (Matthew 5:4). It is very healthy to express the feelings and pain of grief, for then it becomes mourning.

There is comfort to be found in the expression of emotional pain, in putting words to our grief. However, most of us were not taught to mourn in healthy ways. We were taught to accumulate things in life. We were taught to get a good education, get additional education, get a good job, get a house, get a car, get a bigger house, get things to go into that house, get, get, get. We were programmed to be "getters." We were not taught to deal with loss in life. We were not taught to deal with changes in life. We were taught to tough our way through the hard times, to be strong, even to be strong for others.

Sitting beside the bed of her terminally ill husband, the devoted wife is aware of her deep sadness. She is grieving the impending loss of her mate, along with several other losses associated with this relationship. She observes changes on a daily basis.

Suddenly she realizes that her husband is also grieving. He is losing his health, his wife, his children,

his grandchildren, his friends, his home, his possessions, his dreams, and his plans. We grieve the loss of
anything valuable to us, and since we grieve change,
it makes sense that care-receivers are grieving at this
time also.

There were grievers at the foot of the cross. Mary
was losing her son, and John and the other disciples
were losing their hope, their teacher and guide. The
followers of Jesus were losing their miracle worker
and their Messiah.

But, the One on the cross was a griever also.
Although Christ knew the will of His Father was for
Him to be the sacrificial lamb and for Him to die on
the cross for the sins of the world, it meant the end of
His earthly ministry. His grief around this change is
revealed by His words in the Garden of Gethsemane
as He prayed:

> Father, if you are willing, take this cup from me;
> yet not my will, but yours be done.
>
> Luke 22:42

Grief is not a sin. Grief is the normal and natural
response to loss. God put within His creation the

ability to love, to care, and to feel pain and emotions when relationships change.

The role of caregiving is exhausting enough without the added stress of suppressing the grief we feel within. The tools found within these pages are designed to be a guide for expressing these feelings, a guide to help caregivers and care-receivers to mourn in healthy ways. "The Caregiver Bill of Rights" reminds caregivers to create the proper perspective as they perform their difficult task (Appendix B).

Caregivers, care-receivers, and family members should be given permission to grieve and mourn openly. When grief and mourning are expressed, everyone joins the company of the Ultimate Caregiver, Jesus Christ.

THE WORDS OF FORGIVENESS

Two other men, both criminals, were also led out with him to be executed. When they came to the place called the Skull, there they crucified him, along with the criminals—one on his right, the other on his left. Jesus said, "Father, forgive them, for they do not know what they are doing." And they divided up his clothes by casting lots.

Luke 23:32–34

This statement from the Son of God stands out to us because it is so difficult to comprehend due to our humanness. Surely He did not mean this! Forgive them for accusing Him? Forgive them for arresting Him? Forgive them for mocking Him? Forgive them for nailing Him to the cross? Forgive them? Only God in flesh could make such a statement.

To forgive in this context means to let go, to give up a debt, to disregard, to keep no longer. Christ is asking His Heavenly Father to let them get by with it! The ultimate picture of God in flesh, the ultimate gift to the world, is forgiveness.

FORGIVENESS DEFINED

The reluctance to forgive others places the burden upon the one holding the grudge. Holding grudges, feelings of resentment, even bitterness, can take a toll upon the physical, emotional, and spiritual aspects of a person.

A good definition of forgiveness is giving up the hope of a different or better yesterday. Whether yesterday is twenty-four hours ago, or twenty years in the past, it will always be the same. Yesterday will never be any different than it is right now. We can't impact what happened yesterday; we can only waste our time today even trying to do so. Giving up the hope of a different yesterday is not saying something was right or wrong; it is not placing blame upon anyone. This statement is simply saying we must realize things that occurred in the past will always be the same. We cannot change the events of the past even one small amount.

The disciples of Jesus asked Him to teach them to pray:

> He said to them, "When you pray, say: "Father, hallowed be your name, your kingdom come. Give us each day our daily bread. Forgive us our sins, for we also forgive everyone who sins against us. And lead us not into temptation."
>
> Luke 11:2–4

Christ used this as an opportunity to teach the importance of forgiveness. He taught His disciples to seek forgiveness for their own sins, but also to forgive others who have sinned against them. Notice Jesus did not say "for we also forgive everyone who sins against us ... if they say they are sorry ... and if they ask us to forgive them." He provided the example for us. He asked His heavenly Father to forgive those who had not even asked to be forgiven or had expressed any remorse for their actions.

He taught us how to treat our enemies and respond to those who despitefully use us when He said, "But I tell you: Love your enemies and pray for those who persecute you" (Matthew 5:44).

This is exactly what Christ was doing from the cross. He prayed for those who beat Him, falsely accused Him, mocked Him, ridiculed Him, spit upon Him, even crucified Him. He had spoken about forgiving others during His Sermon on the Mount. Now He is the living example of forgiving others while on Golgotha's mount.

It is so much easier to love our friends than it is to love our enemies. Christ, the Ultimate Caregiver, provides the perfect example of praying for those who persecuted Him. His prayer was not pleading God's wrath to be poured upon His enemies, but for God's forgiveness to cover them as a blanket.

> Forgiveness is not always easy. At times, it feels more painful than the wound we suffered, to forgive the one that inflicted it. And yet, there is no peace without forgiveness.
>
> Marianne Williamson

Unfortunately, we live in a world where hateful words are spoken, and hurtful actions are taken against us. It is very difficult to forgive these words and acts, especially when there seems to be no remorse. What would Jesus do? It's obvious. Jesus forgave those who showed no remorse. Even in the midst of the scorn, He asked His Father to forgive them.

THE FORGIVENESS PHRASE

There are five words linked together, a simple phrase, that could change the world if used often. This phrase can bring significant changes to our life and our relationships. The phrase?

I'm sorry, please forgive me.

These are five of the most difficult words to say in the English language. Yet, speaking these words to another person can open the door to reconciliation, and to forgiveness. It is not saying who is wrong or right. This is not a judgmental statement. It is an acknowledgement that it hurts to be estranged or separated in a relationship and that you are seeking to renew the closeness. It is acknowledging personal responsibility and expressing sensitivity to the pain in a relationship. It is extending your heart to meet the heart of another. It is extending your hurt to meet the hurt of another. It takes a lot of courage. It takes trust. It takes the Ultimate Caregiver.

Is there someone needing to hear these words from you? Are there differences to be reconciled with someone? Taking the first step to renew the relationship is the only thing you have control of. Make this statement in person if possible. Or call them so they can hear this phrase. Or send a card to express your heart. I'm sorry, please forgive me. This is a very powerful statement just waiting to be expressed. It is a statement that can begin to heal differences in a relationship.

THE COAT

So, how do we do this? How do we experience God's kind of forgiveness? How does this example of Christ and forgiveness relate to where we are today?

Picture this: at your feet there is a heavy coat. It is oversized, ugly, smelly, and offensive even to look upon. This coat is our un-forgiveness, our attitude, our grudge, our resentment, even our bitterness. Imagine reaching down to pick up this heavy coat while making this statement: "I am putting on this heavy coat of un-forgiveness, resentment, and bitterness because someone has hurt me deeply. I am going to wear it each day of my life. I will live with it, sleep with it, eat with it, and wear it even if it does weigh me down and exhaust me. I am aware that this heavy coat, this load of un-forgiveness, will have a negative impact upon my life. Day after day I will pay a price physically, emotionally, mentally, and spiritually."

Now imagine removing this offensive coat while making the following statement: "I am removing this heavy coat of un-forgiveness, resentment, and bitterness. I am taking it off. I will forgive those who have hurt me because the past will never be any different. I choose to lay aside this burden and not be controlled by events of my past."

Now, picture yourself laying this heavy coat, this burden, at the feet of Jesus and walking away from it. If you ever want to pick this coat up again and wear it, you must come to the feet of Jesus to get it. You must approach the one who taught us to forgive everyone who sins against us. To retrieve this ugly coat of unforgiveness, resentment, and bitterness you must face the Ultimate Caregiver.

> Humble yourselves, therefore, under God's mighty hand, that he may lift you up in due time. Cast all your anxiety on him because he cares for you.

> I Peter 5:6–7

GUILT AND REGRET

Are you feeling guilty about something? Do you regret things that were said or done in a relationship? Both guilt and regret are very normal feelings, especially as we look back over a relationship.

But, there is a difference between guilt and regret. Guilt can come following an intentional action to do or say something. There was a conscious decision made, and then the decision was carried out. This can lead to a feeling of guilt when the relationship changes or ends prematurely.

Regrets can come when there was not a conscious decision involved. It is just the way things happened. Life happened. If you could go back and change the actions and the events, you would do it. But, there is no going back. Remember, forgiveness is giving up the hope of a different or better yesterday.

SPEED BUMPS

Have you ever driven across a parking lot and hit a little speed bump placed there to control the speed of traffic? No matter the speed we are traveling, it hurts. It shakes everything within us. We decide immediately to slow down and watch for speed bumps because it hurt too much and we do not want that to happen again.

Every relationship has its share of speed bumps. Things can happen in relationships that shakes everything within us. These speed bumps may be a lack of communication, broken promises, loss of trust, neglect, poor choices, oversight, etc. When these events occur we usually decide to slow down and pay closer attention to the relationship. Hitting the speed bump hurt too much, and we don't want it to happen again. The pain of the event may cause us to be more sensitive to others and anticipate the impact of our choices. We begin to recognize the speed bumps and make deliberate adjustments to avoid the pain.

It is so easy to live life without consideration of others and the impact our decisions might have on them. We are often so focused on making a living that we overlook the important things in life. It is true: the important things in life are not things at all ... they are relationships.

When faced with a crisis in life, a chronic or terminal illness, the loss of a valuable relationship, the failure of a dream, or a hundred other life events ... the entire picture can change. Priorities in life change. What was once very important to us in life can move to the bottom of the priority list. Also, those things that seemed to always be the least important things to us have a way of suddenly moving to the top of the list. Our perspective on life the way we view it, changes. This might be a great time for us to slow down ... to watch for speed bumps in the relationships we treasure.

"FATHER, FORGIVE THEM"

In a love so unimaginable
Through eyes of mercy,
He prayed, "Father, forgive them,
These ones you've given me."

"I came as You instructed
Out of obedience to You
To accomplish what they could not
And do for them what they can't do."

"I walked their paths, I took their place,
Their sin was placed on Me,
And now I die so they might live,
Forgiven and set free."

"Unleash what chains might bind them
From burdens they may bear
So that forgiveness now they walk in
Is the same as what they share."

"Stir love within their hearts
To reach to their fellow man

As they continue what I started
In spreading love the best they can."

"Let them see beyond this life
To know there's heavenly gates
Open wide for them to walk through
With Your arms open wide that wait."

©09/2007 D. Golden Boyd

PERSONAL NOTES

_____

_____

_____

_____

_____

_____

_____

_____

_____

_____

THE WORDS OF FAITH

One of the criminals who hung there hurled insults at him: "Aren't you the Christ? Save yourself and us!"

But the other criminal rebuked him. "Don't you fear God," he said, "since you are under the same sentence? We are punished justly, for we are getting what our deeds deserve. But this man has done nothing wrong."

Then he said, "Jesus, remember me when you come into your kingdom."

Jesus answered him, "I tell you the truth, today you will be with me in paradise."

Luke 23:39–43

The response of Christ to the thief on the cross next to Him holds a tremendous truth for those facing a crisis in life. Today actually means immediately, instant, right away. Christ would not have made this statement if there was any delay in the process. If there were another step along the route to heaven, Christ would have mentioned it here.

The key to heaven, to paradise, is found here. Out of a request of remember me came the expression of hope from the Son of God. For the thief hanging on the cross, his mouth and throat scorching from the heat of the sun, parched from the fever, paradise was a promise of relief, a garden of fruit trees, shade, fountains of clear water, and true happiness.

Even in His hour of torment, Christ extended hope to the hopeless, grace to the greedy, salvation to the sinner, faith to the forgiven.

This statement from Christ is clear evidence that works do not save us, only our faith in Christ will save us. It is never too late to turn to God. It is never too late to join the thief on the cross in saying remember me.

This condemned thief was never able to attend a church service, never able to contribute to the budget of a church, never taught a class, or served on a church committee. But, his simple statement of faith ushered him into the comfort and peace of paradise.

The only baptism the dying thief knew was the baptism of the Holy Spirit of God while hanging upon the cross next to His Saviour. His only Holy Communion was being an eyewitness to the broken body next to him. He recognized the blood flowing from Christ as the sacrifice of the unblemished and perfect Lamb of God.

> For it is by grace you have been saved, through faith—and this not from yourselves, it is the gift of God—not by works, so that no one can boast.
>
> Ephesians 2:8–9

INSTANT SALVATION

We live in an instant society. We want our computer to be the fastest available; we pop our food into a microwave and grow impatient if it takes more than a minute to prepare. We want everything in our life to be instant: instant coffee, instant soup, instant oatmeal, instant credit, instant messages, and on and on ... instantly. We even use the remote control to surf channels during commercials because they seem to be wasting our precious time! We want instant gratification, instant results.

The conversation between Christ and the thief hanging next to him reveals the greatest news in the world. We can have instant salvation! One thief was mocking Christ, joining his voice in chorus with those who were also ridiculing Him. The penitent thief recognized the Holy One hanging on the cross. During these hours of shame and disgrace, his sinfulness was exposed as it was contrasted to the purity and innocence of the sinless one next to him. "Jesus, remember me ... " he uttered. What a marvelous statement from a thief to the Son of God, from a sinner to the Perfect One, from one who took from others to the One who offers life as a free gift to the world.

> Come now, let us reason together, says the LORD. Though your sins are like scarlet, they shall be as white as snow; though they are red as crimson, they shall be like wool.
>
> Isaiah 1:18

The cross is recognized around the world as the symbol of God's love, God's mercy, God's patience, God's forgiveness, and God's perfect plan. It has been the central theme of songs, books, poems, and artwork. It was not just God's Son being crucified; it was the Ultimate Caregiver hanging on the cross.

The Gospel writers bear witness to an event that is the foundation of hope for all mankind. The death of Christ on the cross was the sacrificial shedding of blood for the sins of man. God's only Son, the Chosen One, the Messiah, was sent to become the atonement for man, the payment for sins.

But, there is something that God does not have. God does not have a Plan B! He does not have a backup plan for man's salvation. He was not caught off guard with the death of Christ. He was not sent into a panic because of the events of Calvary's cross. The death of Christ was God's Plan A for man's redemption. It was then, it is still, and always will be His Plan A.

There is a fountain filled with blood,
Drawn from Immanuel's veins,
And sinners plunged beneath that flood,
Lose all their guilty stains.
The dying thief rejoiced to see
That fountain in his day.
And there may I, as vile as he,
Wash all my sins away.
William Cowper

THE WAY TO LIFE

For all have sinned and fall short of the glory of God.

Romans 3:23

For the wages of sin is death, but the gift of God is eternal life in Christ Jesus our Lord.

Romans 6:23

For everyone who calls on the name of the Lord will be saved.

Romans 10:13

If we confess our sins, He is faithful and just and will forgive us our sins and purify us from all unrighteousness.

I John 1:9

Here I am! I stand at the door and knock. If anyone hears my voice and opens the door, I will come in and eat with him, and he with me.

Revelation 3:20

Because of the urgency of time, the thief was only able to voice remember me. God honored the intent of his heart, even more than the words. If speaking a certain phrase would guarantee us of heaven, those who could not speak would be doomed forever. If doing good works would usher us into heaven, those too weak to stand would be among the hopeless. But God has a better plan, a plan of faith, one of trust.

A brief prayer is found below, no magic words, nothing but a simple prayer of faith. Would you consider praying this prayer? Do these words express the desire of your heart?

God, I confess that I am a sinner. I believe the Lord Jesus Christ died for my sins. I do now receive and confess Him as my Lord and Savior. By faith I trust you to forgive my sins, cleanse me, and surround me with your love. Bring healing to my broken heart. Amen

Caregivers, find some private time to discuss the information above with your care-receiver. This should be approached in a sensitive way, not in judgment or confrontation. Write their responses so they will be recorded for future reference.

Also, offer to contact a spiritual leader they are comfortable with if they have questions or would like more information on this issue. Always seek to leave the lines of communication open with the care-receiver. Trust the Ultimate Caregiver to lead you, to guide you, and to strengthen you at this time.

A TESTIMONY OUTLINE

What have you done with Christ? Are you able to share the testimony of Christ in your life? Spend time to discuss and express answers to these questions:

What was your life like without Christ? (your natural state)

_____

_____

_____

_____

_____

_____

_____

_____

How did you come to know Christ? What happened?
(your conversion)

_____

_____

_____

_____

_____

_____

_____

How is your life different with Christ? (your testimony)

_____

_____

_____

_____

_____

_____

_____

_____

Share these responses with loved ones. Write them down for future generations to reflect upon your spiritual journey and witness. As you express the assurance of your salvation to family and friends, it becomes a treasure of comfort to them. Rejoice in God's plan, and reaffirm your belief in His promises. Use God's Word to gain strength, faith, comfort, guidance, and assurance in God's power to save, keep, and encourage you. To assist you in this journey, please see "Searching the Scriptures" (Appendix C).

KEEP YOUR SUITCASE PACKED

This account of a daughter being the caregiver for her ailing mother is significant because of the truth it contains:

My Mama was getting tired. She had been sick

for a long time, confined to a bed for months. She was ready to go. I wasn't as ready, but Mama was ready to go see Jesus.

I crawled up in the bed with Mama, held her like she had hugged her little girl so many years before. I could feel her shallow breathing, and it was as if I could detect each bone in her frail body.

"Mama, I am not ready for you to go," I quietly said.

"I know, baby doll, but I'm ready," said Mama. "The Lord is ready for me, real soon."

"But Mama, I want to go with you," I said, as I gazed into her eyes.

"Honey, you can't go with me; it's my turn to go, not your turn yet," Mama said. "But keep your suitcase packed; you will come see me again when it's your time. Just keep your suitcase packed."

Those words from Mama have stuck with me over the years. Yes, I still miss her; I still shed tears when I miss her, and I still laugh aloud when I remember some of the things she did. But, the most valuable truth Mama taught me was to keep my suitcase packed. I'll see Mama again someday in heaven; I just don't know when that will be. But when the Lord comes for me, He will find me waiting … with my suitcase packed.

The process of normal aging or a disease progression demands our attention to the physical needs. We surround ourselves with experts, seeking the latest medical advancements and treatments. We will invest our last dollar into the goal of physical wholeness.

Because of the brevity and uncertainty of life, it is imperative for each of us to make preparations in the spiritual aspect of life. Since there are no guarantees in life, not even assured of our next heartbeat, the importance of a solid spiritual component is essential for peace in life. James put it into focus for us as he wrote:

> Now listen, you who say, "Today or tomorrow we will go to this or that city, spend a year there, carry on business and make money." Why, you do not even know what will happen tomorrow. What is your life? You are a mist that appears for a little while and then vanishes. Instead, you ought to say, "If it is the Lord's will, we will live and do this or that."
>
> James 4:13–15

If you are reading this material, God has given you an opportunity to find peace in Him. Like the thief on the cross, our prayer could simply be "remember me." The thief packed his suitcase, made spiritual preparation while the opportunity was before him. Have you packed your suitcase? Now is the perfect time to approach the Ultimate Caregiver.

CAN THEY SEE US?

A very common question asked in grief support groups is "Can our loved ones in Heaven see us?" This is a great question, and it seems the Scriptures provide the answer for us.

Hebrews chapter eleven is known as the Faith Hall of Fame. Names of faithful people in the Bible are listed there: Abel, Enoch, Noah, Abraham, Isaac, Jacob, Joseph, Moses, Rahab, Gideon, Barak, Samson, Jephthah, David, Samuel, the prophets, and many other references. The common ingredient mentioned in this chapter is their faith in God.

Then the twelfth chapter of Hebrews continues the writer's thought:

> Therefore, since we are surrounded by such a great cloud of witnesses, let us throw off everything that hinders and the sin that so easily entangles, and let us run with perseverance the race marked out for us. Let us fix our eyes on Jesus, the author and perfecter of our faith, who for the joy set

before him endured the cross, scorning its shame, and sat down at the right hand of the throne of God. Consider him who endured such opposition from sinful men, so that you will not grow weary and lose heart.

Hebrews 12:1–3

What a tremendous statement in the Scriptures. The writer is saying the characters mentioned in the previous chapter, those in the Faith Hall of Fame, are circled about us watching our every move. Wow! What a humbling thought. People in heaven can see our every action. They witness our good deeds and our not so good deeds.

Before that statement frightens you too much, consider this. Our loved ones who have gone on to heaven are in a place where there is no heartache, no sorrow, no tears, no sadness, no death. So, even though they are witnesses to our earthly lives, they cannot feel sorrow for our trials or sins. We cannot break their heart by our actions or words. If we could break the heart of those in heaven, then it would not be heaven!

And I heard a loud voice from the throne saying, "Now the dwelling of God is with men, and he

will live with them. They will be his people, and
God himself will be with them and be their God.
He will wipe every tear from their eyes. There will
be no more death or mourning or crying or pain,
for the old order of things has passed away."

Revelation 21:3–4

Our loved ones in Heaven realize our time on earth,
less than a century in most cases, is just a blip on the
radar screen. We look at our lives, limited as they are
in years. They look at eternity with no limit on time.
They are focused on eternity with loved ones and Our
Lord, the Ultimate Caregiver.

"YOU WERE GRIEVING, TOO"

I thought of all you lost, as I
allowed myself to grieve,
Of everything you said good bye to,
when you knew you had to leave.

There was your physical ability, that was taken away
As you found yourself con-
fined, mostly in a chair all day.

There was a future you had planned,
to bring long-awaited peace
That was no longer promised, because
of pain with no release.

There was golf you couldn't play,
where you had such fun
And now you couldn't hope to get,
that sought after hole-in-one.
There were grandkids growing up,
that you knew you wouldn't see,
And growing old together, like you
thought you'd do with me.

There were goals your own kids made,
that now you wouldn't know
With time running out for you,
before you knew you had to go.

So, as I grieve in losing one, I know
you grieved much more

Bravely facing the unknown, and leaving memories of before.

I wished I would have talked about
those fears you must have had
Instead of centering on myself, in
the pain that made me sad.

Because in all the many losses,
you were going through
You had much to say good bye to,
as I tried to give up you.
Perhaps I can take the courage, like I saw you display
In living with my greatest loss, with-
out you with me every day.

©02/12/1999 D. Golden Boyd

PERSONAL NOTES

_____

_____

_____

THE WORDS OF PROVISION

Near the cross of Jesus stood his mother, his mother's sister, Mary the wife of Clopas, and Mary Magdalene. When Jesus saw his mother there, and the disciple whom he loved standing nearby, he said to his mother, "Dear woman, here is your son," and to the disciple, "Here is your mother." From that time on, this disciple took her into his home.

John 19:25–27

What a beautiful statement from the Son of God. He was providing for His mother while the life blood was pouring from His wounds. Among those at the foot of the cross were Mary, His mother's sister, Mary the wife of Clopas, Mary Magdalene, and the disciple Jesus loved dearly…John. His words actually mean "Son, look upon your mother; mother, look upon your son." Jesus requested His beloved disciple to care for his mother. From that very moment John took Mary under his wing to provide comfort and protection. Christ was fulfilling His role as the Ultimate Caregiver.

THE EXAMPLE OF CHRIST

This passage is an excellent example of Christ practicing what He preached. While hanging on the cross, enduring the pain of torture, with His life blood seeping from His body, He was thinking of others. His obedience to be nailed to the cross honored His Father. From the cross He honors His mother by making provision for her welfare after His death.

A loose translation could be "John, take care of my mother, provide for her, comfort her, and treat her as your own mother." This was Christ taking care of His family before His death. We are no different. Just as we spend our lives providing care for our loved ones, it is also a paramount need for us to address at the end of life. When faced with a life-threatening illness, we begin to seriously address the important issues of wills, estates, trusts, investments, deeds, personal possessions, etc.

We make intentional efforts during life to expand and enlarge our circle of friends, developing close relationships and seeking new ones. As our physical condition changes, there seems to be a reverse in this trend. The circle of close friends draws smaller and closer. It is necessary to identify supportive relationships from those already established. It takes energy and time to develop close and supportive relationships. During these times of change and uncertainty it may be too difficult to invest the effort into building new relationships. Immediate family members and close friends may be called upon to provide the necessary care and comfort.

This time of caregiving presents a unique opportunity for family and friends to express feelings of love, appreciation, forgiveness, and support. Years of providing the physical, emotional, and spiritual support for a loved one are called upon to reach a new level. The wedding vows of in sickness and health can become a reality now. There is a call to put actions to the words, to allow the expressions of love to extend beyond the words.

EXPRESSIONS OF SUPPORT

Physical support can be provided by caregivers through their thoughtfulness, kindness, anticipating the needs, applying a wet cloth on the forehead, or rubbing lotion on the feet, hands and back. These comfort measures, the human touch, are gifts of mercy and compassion.

Emotional support can also be provided by caregivers during this time, although it is often overlooked. This is a time for listening, acknowledging the words of a loved one as they take inventory of their life. This is not a time to judge or confront, but a time for supportive presence. Comforting one another, crying together, and expressing feelings from the heart are important aspects of emotional support.

Spiritual support can be provided by caregivers through prayer, reading favorite passages of Scripture from the Bible, perhaps poetry or an excerpt from a favorite book. An alternative to reading is to play an audio recording of a favorite author or minister.

A comforting support during this time for many is to have Gospel music or hymns playing softly in the background. If music was an important part of life for someone, it may be very soothing at this time also.

Our loved one, the care-receiver, may also feel the need to address these aspects of physical, emotional, and spiritual support. It may be extremely important for them to have someone write their wishes in these days. Prized possessions may be given to certain family members, and a list of final details might need to be completed.

The opportunity for loved ones to spend time together, alone, in a private setting can be very important. A critically ill person might need to share intimately with a child, regardless of their age. "Take care of your mother," "stay close to your sister," "move closer to the kids," and hundreds of other heartfelt requests have been uttered at thousands of bedsides. These expressions of love and providing for the welfare of loved ones are reflections of the words of Christ from the cross as He cared for His own mother. Regardless of the content expressed, it is very important to provide the opportunity for family members to spend private and uninterrupted time together. This provides a gift of time, a blessing of words, and an exchange of hearts.

Therefore, as God's chosen people, holy and

dearly loved, clothe yourselves with compassion, kindness, humility, gentleness and patience. Bear with each other and forgive whatever grievances you may have against one another. Forgive as the Lord forgave you.

Colossians 3:12–13

ORGANIZING FEELINGS

During a time of grief and change, our feelings and emotions are very erratic, difficult to control, even unclear and confusing at times. Use the following guide to organize these feelings. Express yourself as openly and honestly as possible, write from your heart. Imagine you had the opportunity to express the feelings of your heart to your loved one.

I want to thank you for:

_____

_____

_____

_____

_____

My fondest memory of you is:

_____

_____

_____

_____

_____

I want to apologize to you for:

_____

_____

_____

_____

_____

I forgive you for:

_____

_____

_____

_____

_____

I hurt when I think of:

_____

_____

_____

_____

_____

I feel good when I think of:

_____

_____

_____

_____

_____

I feel guilty because of:

_____

_____

_____

_____

_____

I regret:

_____

_____

_____

_____

_____

I would like to hear you say:

_____

_____

_____

_____

_____

I want you to know:

_____

_____

_____

_____

_____

This guide for organizing feelings can be shared with a loved one during daily conversation. Perhaps discussing one of these components each day will encourage your loved one to express their feelings also. Trust the leadership of the Ultimate Caregiver to provide the time, the courage, and the guidance for this expression.

MISSED OPPORTUNITIES

It has been said that the Greeks had a god for everything, a sculpture or bust to express every feeling known to man. The god of opportunity was portrayed by the bust of a man with a long shaggy beard, and a mustache that covered his mouth. His eyebrows were full and bushy, hanging over his eyes. He had long shaggy hair that was constantly covering his face. But, from his ears back…he had no hair…he was slick bald from the middle of his head. The entire back of his head had no hair at all. This was an image of the god of opportunity. The meaning is simple: when an opportunity comes your way, you must grasp it from the front…for once an opportunity passes you, there is nothing to hold onto! Have you ever missed an opportunity by not grasping it while it was in front of you? Perhaps we have all learned our greatest lessons by staring at opportunities from the backside, when there is nothing to grasp.

Look for the opportunity to share your expressions, perhaps to your loved one, or to another safe person. A safe person is someone who will lend you their ears, and not their mouth. You do not need advice, you do not need to be judged for what you feel or say. You need someone who will patiently listen as you express your heart.

"SON, BEHOLD THY MOTHER ... "

Even hanging on the cross
And just before He died,
Jesus gave John to His mother,
Then placed her at His brother's side.

It was example how in leaving.
His love and care are shown
In handing one off to the other
So that they were not left alone.

And He works the same today
In the very ones He sends
With comfort He leaves us
Through families and friends.

The love they have inside them
That they reach out to share
Is His own that works to reach us
And keep us in His care.

It's His way of being with us
In their kind word and good deed,
Shown in those He sends
To see to our every need.

We are never left abandoned
To walk life's pathways on our own
When those He places bring His presence
To make sure we're aren't alone.

©09/2007 D. Golden Boyd

PERSONAL NOTES

_____

_____

_____

_____

_____

_____

_____

_____

_____

_____

_____

_____

_____

_____

_____

_____

_____

_____

THE WORDS OF QUESTIONING

At the sixth hour darkness came over the whole land until the ninth hour. And at the ninth hour Jesus cried out in a loud voice, "Eloi, Eloi, lama sabachthani?"—which means, "My God, my God, why have you forsaken me?"

Mark 15:33–34

These words of Christ are expressing His feelings of being abandoned, deserted, being left hopeless and helpless. He became sin for all of mankind; the weight of the world's sin was upon Him. God does not, He will not, He cannot, embrace sin.

> My God, my God, why have you forsaken me?
> Why are you so far from saving me,
> so far from the words of my groaning?
> O my God, I cry out by day, but you do not answer,
> by night, and am not silent.

Psalms 22:1–2

These words of Christ, the expression of being abandoned, come after He endured three hours of darkness while hanging on the cross. Christ had claimed to be the Light of the World, and He had just hung through three hours of darkness. The darkness represented the sinfulness of mankind. Christ was taking the sins of the world upon Himself, and God was not able to look upon sin. The One who became sin for us felt as if God had turned His back upon Him. He felt deserted in His hour of need, abandoned when He needed support and strength. He felt a tremendous separation from His Heavenly Father because of the darkness that fell upon Calvary's cross.

He expressed the aching of His heart, the feeling of being left alone to suffer in agony.

"My God, My God, Why have you forsaken me?"

It is quite common for caregivers to feel abandoned or deserted by loved ones during a time when support would be valued. When it would be extremely helpful to have assistance to carry the heavy emotional and physical load, there is often a feeling of being forsaken by family and friends. Resentment, blaming others, feeling trapped in a situation, even a feeling of not being appreciated for the sacrifices being made, are prevalent feelings of caregivers. It breaks the heart.

Loved ones, the care-receivers, can experience similar feelings. It is bad enough to have a chronic or terminal illness. But to be struggling each day with the physical changes is made even worse when it seems no one cares. The lack of support and encouragement provided to them in hours of need can cause caregivers and their loved ones to identify with this statement from Christ, a feeling of abandonment. Even the Ultimate Caregiver felt unappreciated, abandoned, and rejected.

ASKING WHY

Is it okay to ask why? When we are faced with a disease that is life threatening, we need permission to ask why. Caregivers who are watching loved ones struggle need permission each day to ask why.

Here is a great example set for us. The Son of God, the sinless one, asked why. He felt forsaken. If Christ could express His humanness, surely we should be able to express it also.

Phyllis, a dear friend of mine, was the caregiver for her fiancée, Pat, during his terminal illness. He was constantly asking "Why me? Why us? Why now? Why not someone else?" After days of hearing these recurring questions, Phyllis responded with, "God only knows why. And He hasn't told me yet. As soon as He tells me why, I'll tell you." They shared laughter at her statement, but it provided a safe way for Pat to voice his frustrations. Her response was very accurate and provided an honest response to his questions.

Care-receivers, our loved ones, need a safe place to express their feelings of being abandoned. They also need a safe person who will exhibit patience and understanding when we need to ask why? Phyllis was right, God only knows why.

It is easy to feel forsaken by friends, even by family,

during a time of personal crisis. Most people do not know what to say. They may be afraid of saying the wrong thing, or perhaps the experience reminds them of a painful experience in their own life. Caregivers and care-receivers may sense others staying away during this time. It hurts to feel abandoned during this time of need.

Christ questioned why His Father had forsaken or abandoned Him. But in reality, many of His disciples and followers had also abandoned Him. How much did it hurt for Judas to turn on Him, for Peter to deny Him, for His disciples to stand afar off during His arrest, His trial, and His crucifixion? He felt abandoned at His time of need.

> From this time many of his disciples turned back and no longer followed him. "You do not want to leave too, do you?" Jesus asked the Twelve. Simon Peter answered him, "Lord, to whom shall we go? You have the words of eternal life. We believe and know that you are the Holy One of God."
>
> John 6:66–69

Job knew what it felt like to be abandoned while going through trials in life. His children had died, he had lost his possessions, and he was covered with a loathsome skin disease. It was in the midst of his abandonment that he exclaimed:

> He has alienated my brothers from me; my acquaintances are completely estranged from me. My kinsmen have gone away; my friends have forgotten me. My guests and my maidservants count me a stranger; they look upon me as an alien. I summon my servant, but he does not answer, though I beg him with my own mouth. My breath is offensive to my wife; I am loathsome to my own brothers. Even the little boys scorn me; when I appear, they ridicule me. All my intimate friends detest me; those I love have turned against me.
>
> Job 19:13–19

It can be easy for depression and discouragement to set in. Situations seem to be helpless, life doesn't seem to be fair, the future doesn't seem to be bright. There seems to be no encouragement. It seems no one cares. Everyone is going on with their lives and schedules without any thought of where things might be with the caregivers and care-receivers right now.

This can be a time to ask why, not a time to give up. There is a difference. God can use this time to draw you close to Him, to speak softly to your heart, to give direction and encouragement, even in the midst of the darkness.

> The Christian life is not a constant high. I have my moments of deep discouragement. I have to go to God in prayer with tears in my eyes, and say, "O God, forgive me!" or "Help Me."
>
> Billy Graham

Corrie Ten Boom was a young girl living with her family in Holland during the Second World War. Their home became a hiding place, a refuge, for fugitives and those hunted by the Nazis. Corrie and several members of her family were arrested for their deeds, and sent to a Nazi concentration camp. She survived this ordeal, realizing that her faith in God had spared her. The remainder of her life was spent proclaiming the message of Jesus Christ as the Liberator.

Even though Corrie Ten Boom faced danger and uncertainty, she continued to cling to her faith in the Ultimate Caregiver.

When a train goes through a tunnel and it gets
dark, you don't throw away the ticket and jump
off. You sit still and trust the engineer.

Corrie Ten Boom

You may feel this is a very dark time for you in life. It
may be extremely difficult to even see the next minute, impossible to see into tomorrow. The caregiving
role can be a very lonely role, often unappreciated by
family and friends. Those we expected to be present are often scarce, and seemingly limited in their
availability.

But, don't give up. Don't throw away your ticket
and jump off. This is a time to look for encouragement from the Lord. Look for that person He has
placed into your life just to provide support and
encouragement during this time in your life. Nothing
ever surprises God, so He must have a plan to work
everything out to honor Him. After all, He is the
Ultimate Caregiver .

THE WHY LIST

Make a list of why questions. Write them down; exhaust your mind of every question. Add to this list each time another why crosses your mind. Realize that in expressing these questions, you are joining the company of thousands, even millions, who have asked the same questions. Notice also that even the Son of God asked His heavenly Father this question. Yet even Christ, the Ultimate Caregiver, did not receive an answer.

Why?

_____

_____

_____

_____

_____

_____

_____

IDENTIFYING SUPPORTIVE PEOPLE

A supportive person will be someone who accepts you without being judgmental. They let you describe your feelings, and they understand your life circumstances and how they impact each area of your life. They are at your side, supporting you to do whatever is important and best for you, and your loved one. They will allow you to ask why without feeling they must provide an answer.

List the people who make up your support system. Identify the safe people who will be available to you physically, emotionally, and spiritually. Write their name and telephone numbers on these lines.

_____

_____

_____

_____

_____

_____

_____

_____

THE ROLLER COASTER

Being a caregiver, or a care-receiver, is like riding a roller coaster. Most people can ride a roller coaster, some more comfortable with it than others, if they can hold onto the seat and scream at the top of their lungs when it is approaching a drop off!

But caregivers and care-receivers are riding a roller coaster in life ... with a blindfold on. Can you imagine what it would feel like to ride a roller coaster without the ability to see and prepare for the sudden drops or the steep turns?

Being a caregiver for a loved one can be this unpredictable. You cannot predict the changes that might take place today. You cannot brace yourself for the sudden shift in moods, personalities, and physical or mental capabilities. Often these changes seem to come out of nowhere without any warning. They can take your breath away. Major changes can happen in an instant.

Also, you cannot predict or change how other people will respond to your need for support and assistance. When you trust someone to be there for you and they let you down, it is more difficult to trust them the next time.

To help level out the roller coaster during the caregiving process, consider working on this exercise:

Make a list of the changes and decisions that have felt good in the caregiver role:

_____

_____

_____

_____

_____

_____

_____

Make a list of the changes and decisions that have hurt in the caregiver role:

_____

_____

_____

_____

_____

_____

_____

"MY GOD, MY GOD, WHY HAVE YOU FORSAKEN ME?"

Watching endless suffering of a loved one in pain,
I ask, "How much longer, God?"
through what hours remain.

In desperate optimism to seek out something bright,
The answer to, "What I'm to do?"
fails to come to light.

When God appears so distant as if
prayers have gone unheard,
He reminds, "You must have patience
and hold tight to My word."

He says, "There's hope I give you
though you don't clearly see,
And because hope's built on trust,
you must trust in Me."
"Never think that I forget you; I
love you, you are Mine,
What seems delayed in answers falls in My timeline."

"Just as when My Son was hanging, I
heard His anguish when He cried,
'My God, You have forsaken me!' and
I brought life after He died."

"And in my timing, when it's right,
that hope will be revealed to you;
Just wait for Me in patience till all
I need to do is through."

©10/03/2004 D. Golden Boyd

PERSONAL NOTES

_____

_____

_____

_____

_____

_____

_____

THE WORDS OF
SUFFERING

Later, knowing that all was now completed, and so that the Scripture would be fulfilled, Jesus said, "I am thirsty." A jar of wine vinegar was there, so they soaked a sponge in it, put the sponge on a stalk of the hyssop plant, and lifted it to Jesus' lips.

John 19:28–29

To thirst means to suffer from the lack of moisture. Due to the fever and wounds, thirst was evident to the Son of God. He desired to be refreshed, supported, and strengthened.

Can you picture Jesus Christ on the Cross? His entire body was racked with pain, His features swollen and bruised, His brow was punctured by thorns, and His back lacerated from the scourging. Can you hear the blood dripping from where the jagged spikes had pierced His hands and his feet? Can you see the blood trickle from the gaping holes in His hands, making its way down His arms to the elbows and then dripping onto the ground below? The sun was shining again, the heat had returned. While Jesus was dying on the cross, he developed an agonizing thirst. Death by crucifixion was the most painful mode of torture the Romans had conceived. The draining away of blood from the body brings on intensive thirst. The entire body cries out for water.

David, the psalmist, painted a vivid picture of the death of Christ. You can almost feel the excruciating pain, the torture of the body when all moisture is driven from it.

> I am poured out like water, and all my bones are out of joint. My heart has turned to wax, it has melted away within me.
> My strength is dried up like a potsherd, And my tongue sticks to the roof of my mouth; you lay me in the dust of death.
>
> Psalms 22:14–15

EXPRESSIONS OF THIRST

Physical thirst is expected from someone dealing with a serious disease. When a loved one expresses thirst, we immediately attempt to quench their thirst by providing a drink, something to satisfy them. The moisture in a body can be drained from fever, activity, or other factors.

Emotional thirst also needs to be considered during this time. This can be expressed due to the lack of support from family or friends. There can be a famine of support, a longing for comfort. It could be expressed as a thirst, even a hunger, for emotional support.

Spiritual thirst is often overlooked at this time. Note the statement of thirst from Christ followed the question to His heavenly Father of why He was being forsaken. We may thirst for spiritual strength right now, we may thirst for spiritual comfort right now, and we may thirst for God's presence right now. Without the awareness of God in our circumstances, we might thirst for His presence. When our hope seems to be a mirage, we might thirst for His faith to become our faith.

This expression can actually be based upon a need for self-worth. We thirst for assurance that our life counts for something. We might thirst for the awareness that we have made a difference in someone's life. Each of us has a need to feel needed, and when we face uncertainties in life, we may desire acknowledgement from family and friends.

Payne Stewart, a professional golfer who died in a plane crash in 1999, was asked in an interview how he wanted to be remembered. His response was:

> I'm going to a special place when I die, but I want to make sure my life is special while I'm here.

Perhaps care-receivers, our loved ones, are wanting to ask family and friends … "Will you miss me when I am gone?," "Has my life been special to you?" It is important to know that we have touched someone's life in a unique way during our time on earth. It is important for us to find meaning and purpose in life. Someone who can reflect upon the purpose they had in life, a way to see that their life had meaning and significance, will receive greater peace during a life crisis.

THE BABY KILLER

Dolores is a dedicated evening and weekend hospice nurse who responds more frequently than not to late night calls from frantic caregivers. In her words, "We have the privilege to be called to the patient's home in response to a medical problem." One evening she received an emergency call: a patient was very restless, and his pain was out of control, in spite of the usual dose of pain medication. Dolores went to the patient's home and was able to apply her pain management skills to make this gentleman more comfortable.

While she observed him, watching for signs that the medications were taking effect, they started talking about his life. Dolores questioned him about any World War II involvement, judging that he would have been of that generation. He made a comment about being in the Pacific during the war, but seemed anxious to change the subject. She gently encouraged him to tell her more about his military role in the Pacific.

Reluctantly, he disclosed his role as an aircraft technician assigned to a secret mission. One of the planes he serviced was the Inola Gay, the B-52 bomber. The plane he serviced eventually carried the A-bomb dropped over Hiroshima in August of 1945.

He avoided her eyes when he said softly, "People called me a baby killer." His eyes filled quickly with tears, and he began to sob uncontrollably. As those painful words were spoken, Dolores realized the connection. She exclaimed "Oh No! No! You are not a baby killer! You are a baby saver! If that bomb had not been dropped I would not be here tonight! As a child, I was in a Japanese concentration camp for three and a half years. Your actions helped liberate my family and me. If that bomb had not been dropped, we would have died in that camp. Thank you, thank you, thank you."

Wrapped in a tearful hug, they wept together, both realizing a special connection. He exclaimed to her that he finally felt forgiven. The load of guilt and shame was lifted that night. Instead of being reprimanded and attacked for his role, he received acceptance from someone who understood. For over fifty years this man had carried the burden of being called a baby killer, harboring shame for his part in this historic event. He could finally let go of this burden.

That night, thousands of miles and millions of heartaches from the site of that military maneuver, there were tears of joy. She wept with gratitude for this man she considered to be a hero. He wept because

God had provided him with a messenger of forgiveness and comfort.

Only an all-knowing, all-powerful, all-loving God could have worked out all of the details for this reunion. He saw a man struggling with forgiveness and self-worth. He had prepared a certain nurse for him, for this moment. God does not believe in coincidences. This was evidence of a divine appointment. After all, He is the Ultimate Caregiver.

> The purpose of life is not to be happy. It is to be useful, to be honorable, to be compassionate, to have it make some difference that you have lived and lived well.
>
> Ralph Waldo Emerson

ELEMENTS OF THIRST

Use this time to assure loved ones of your presence to provide physical comfort and support to them. Provide emotional comfort to them by sharing how much of an impact and lasting impression they have had upon your life. Finally ask if there is any spiritual concern or need they might have that you can meet for them.

The Lord can satisfy every physical, emotional, or spiritual thirst that mankind might experience. This may be a time He wishes to use loved ones to quench the thirst of the moment, to meet the expressed needs. This can be a time to trust and rely upon the Ultimate Caregiver.

Discuss responses to these statements with your loved one:

PHYSICAL THIRST

What I am thirsting for physically as a caregiver is

_____

_____

_____

What I am thirsting for physically as a care-receiver is

_____

_____

_____

EMOTIONAL THIRST

What I am thirsting for emotionally as a caregiver is

_____

_____

_____

What I am thirsting for emotionally as a care-receiver is

_____

_____

_____

SPIRITUAL THIRST

What I am thirsting for spiritually as a caregiver is

_____

_____

_____

What I am thirsting for spiritually as a care-receiver is

_____

_____

_____

DIVINE APPOINTMENT

Christ had a divine appointment with a woman at the well in Samaria. After a long hot journey across the barren wilderness, His disciples had gone into town and had left Him there to rest until their return.

When a Samaritan woman came to draw water, Jesus said to her, "Will you give me a drink?" (His disciples had gone into the town to buy food.)

The Samaritan woman said to him, "You are a Jew and I am a Samaritan woman. How can you ask me for a drink?" (For Jews do not associate with Samaritans.)

Jesus answered her, "If you knew the gift of God and who it is that asks you for a drink, you would have asked him and he would have given you living water."

"Sir," the woman said, "you have nothing to draw with and the well is deep. Where can you get this living water? Are you greater than our father Jacob, who gave us the well and drank from it himself, as did also his sons and his flocks and herds?"

Jesus answered, "Everyone who drinks this water will be thirsty again, but whoever drinks the water I give him will never thirst. Indeed, the water I give him will become in him a spring of water welling up to eternal life."

The woman said to him, "Sir, give me this water so that I won't get thirsty and have to keep coming here to draw water."

John 4:7–15

How ironic that the One who taught others about the spring of water welling up to eternal life is the One who later expressed thirst from Calvary's cross. The One who quenched the spiritual thirst of others with living water sought in vain to have His own physical thirst quenched.

Divine appointments are arranged by a God who loves us enough to provide comfort, support, and encouragement from unexpected sources. He uses people to serve as His hands, and His messengers.

The term angel actually means a messenger from God. The God of love and mercy will, by Divine appointment, have angels available to quench the varied thirsts of caregivers and their care-receivers.

Look for the angels. Divine appointments are always the work of the Ultimate Caregiver. These divine appointments always bring honor to the Ultimate Caregiver.

"HELP ME, GOD"

I'm feeling so exhausted
From sleep that I have lost,
Broken up in hour segments
Through endless nights I've tossed.

Demands seem ever constant
And confinement closes in,
With this illness taking over
And the body cannot win.

I'm running short on patience
In the tired state I'm in,
I pray for strength to get me through
As each new day begins.
I ask God to give me kinder words
And a more wholesome thought,
In seeing through responsibilities
And doing what I ought.

I want no regrets
As I keep trying to find ways,
To give my love and comfort
Especially in the final days.

God, give strength more than I've got
In order to get through,
That's beyond my capability
And only comes from you.

PERSONAL NOTES

_____

_____

_____

_____

_____

_____

_____

_____

_____

_____

THE WORDS OF COMPLETION

When he had received the drink, Jesus said, "It is finished." With that, he bowed his head and gave up his spirit.

John 19:30

The word finished is the same as paid in full. The sacrifice of Christ on the cross was bringing His earthly ministry to a close. His work was finished; it was completed. Mission accomplished. The suffering and agony of Christ as the sacrifice for the sins of the world was now complete. There would be no more sacrifice for sin.

For God so loved the world that he gave his one and only Son, that whoever believes in him shall not perish but have eternal life. For God did not send his Son into the world to condemn the world, but to save the world through him. Whoever believes in him is not condemned, but whoever does not believe stands condemned already because he has not believed in the name of God's one and only Son.

John 3:16–18

The death of Christ on the cross seals a new agreement (covenant) between God and man. The old agreement (covenant) involved forgiveness of sins through the blood of an animal sacrifice.

Moses took half of the blood and put it in bowls, and the other half he sprinkled on the altar. Then he took the Book of the Covenant and read it to the people. They responded, "We will do everything the LORD has said; we will obey." Moses then took the blood, sprinkled it on the people and said, "This is the blood of the covenant that the LORD has made with you in accordance with all these words."

Exodus 24:6–8

But instead of a spotless lamb on the altar, Jesus offered Himself, the spotless Lamb of God. His sacrifice would forgive sin once and for all. Jesus was the final sacrifice for sins, and His blood sealed the new agreement between God and man. Now we can approach God through Jesus Christ, in full confidence that He will hear us, forgive us, and save us from our sins.

Following the Last Supper with His disciples, Jesus spent time in the Garden of Gethsemane. During this time He predicted His betrayal, He comforted His disciples, and He also promised the indwelling of the Holy Spirit. Contained within this prayer of Jesus is an acknowledgement that He had completed the mission His heavenly Father had assigned to Him.

> After Jesus said this, he looked toward heaven and prayed: "Father, the time has come. Glorify your Son, that your Son may glorify you. For you granted him authority over all people that he might give eternal life to all those you have given him. Now this is eternal life: that they may know you, the only true God, and Jesus Christ, whom you have sent. I have brought you glory on earth by completing the work you gave me to do. And now, Father, glorify me in your presence with the glory I had with you before the world began.
>
> John 17:1–5

The Apostle Paul knew what it was make a total commitment to a cause. He loved Christ, he compelled others to follow Christ, he established churches, and he encouraged believers through his visits and written word. Paul endured hardships, beatings, was stoned, and shipwrecked numerous times. All this he did for the cause of Christ. His commitment to Christ is evident in this statement, "So I will very gladly spend for you everything I have and expend myself as well…" (II Corinthians 12:15).

Paul laid it all on the line for Christ. After he was converted, he dedicated his life to Christ and did not look back. He was bold in his witness and faithful to his beliefs. He expected opposition because of his decision to serve Christ. Paul knew he could place his total trust in the Ultimate Caregiver:

> That is why I am suffering as I am. Yet I am not ashamed, because I know whom I have believed, and am convinced that he is able to guard what I have entrusted to him for that day.
>
> II Timothy 1:12

Paul reached a point in his life when he saw his ministry coming to a close. He was willing to give his life for the cause of Christ. Paul wrote to a young preacher named Timothy, sharing another personal aspect in his writing. Here he makes an intimate confession of his readiness to meet the Lord. He recognized his work was finished, that the time had come for his death.

> For I am already being poured out like a drink offering, and the time has come for my departure. I have fought the good fight, I have finished the race, I have kept the faith. Now there is in store for me the crown of righteousness, which the Lord, the righteous Judge, will award to me on that day—and not only to me, but also to all who have longed for his appearing.
>
> II Timothy 4:6–8

UNFINISHED BUSINESS

As caregivers and care-receivers, look for the opportunity to identify areas of life where there may be some unfinished task or business. There can be a sense of urgency to complete these important steps. Remember, these tasks are being attempted while the concentration level is totally shaken. It is very difficult to even maintain a focus on important daily tasks. Caregivers and care-receivers are living in a fog, walking through each day on automatic pilot. Develop a plan to complete these tasks if at all possible. There may be a need to recruit the assistance of a friend or family member to help accomplish the goals decided upon.

Things that never really seemed important can become a priority during this time of change. When a selected task is completed, realize you have "finished" a very important project. You have lightened the burden for family members.

Make a list of projects you would like to complete. List them in order of priority. Along with each project, list the name of someone you can work with to finish the project.

_____

_____

_____

_____

_____

_____

CHANGING PRIORITIES

Everyone has plans, things they would like to accomplish in life. Some of these plans will have a time frame to work within. Some will not. When faced with a life-changing illness or a major crisis in life, the plans can change. We can't see long term anymore; our outlook is shortened. Important things are put on a fast track. Priorities change!

It is quite common to create a checklist, sometimes written, often not. This checklist is usually created to take care of important decisions first. This might be dealing with financial matters, working through legal documents, wills, trusts, deeds, funeral arrangements, pulling together all of the insurance policies, and other important papers. "Making a Checklist" can provide direction and guidance during this time of confusion and uncertainty (Appendix D).

THE WRAPPER

A fatal heart attack had suddenly removed a man from the family circle who served as husband, father, father-in-law, grandfather, and a multitude of other special relationships. A few days following the funeral service, I met with the family members for a special time of remembrance. We talked about the good memories of the deceased, the happy times shared by the family over the years. These stories brought forth tears of laughter and tears of sorrow. But, nonetheless, it was a time of healing for all involved. It has been stated that when a loved one dies, we lose the physical relationship only; the emotional and spiritual relationships continue to be part of us. In our family meeting, we discovered the healing qualities of sharing precious memories.

A beautiful illustration was given by a daughter-in-law during the family session. I have shared this story many times since, always with a tremendous amount of appreciation for the truth it sets forth. Here is the account as it was shared with me.

Following the death and the funeral service, her four-year-old son came to her and asked, "Where is Grandpa?" She gently told him "Grandpa died." The young boy looked at her even more intently and asked again, "Where is Grandpa?" Suddenly aware of her helpless condition, the young mother responded "Grandpa is in heaven." A look of satisfaction crossed the young boy's face, and he quietly went to bed for the night.

The next morning, the family members drove to the cemetery to see the grave. Everyone got out of the car, walked to the edge of the grave which was completely covered with flowers. The four-year-old boy approached the mound of flowers, turned to his mother and asked, "Is this heaven?"

The mother felt helpless for an answer to the young boy's honest question. How could she explain to him the difference between Grandpa being in heaven, and visiting Grandpa's grave? That evening she sat on the edge of her young son's bed and took a candy bar from her pocket. The boy's eyes lit up as she opened the wrapper to reveal the chocolate treat inside. She broke off a chunk of the candy bar, handed it to the boy and said, "Let's talk about Grandpa. What good memories do you have of Grandpa?"

The excitement was obvious as he told how Grandpa had taken him fishing, they had gone to the zoo together, they had even gone to a baseball game together! The whole time he shared these happy memories, he was enjoying more and more of the candy bar.

As the good memories and the candy bar were finished, the young mother snuggled up close to the boy, gave him a big hug, and said, "You know son, Grandpa is a lot like this candy bar. The good, delicious, wonderful, and enjoyable part of Grandpa that you remember, that's the part of Grandpa that's in heaven."

Then, holding up the empty candy bar wrapper, she said, "This is the part of Grandpa that's buried in the ground...just Grandpa's wrapper."

A look of delight swept over the young boy's face as he realized the enjoyable part of people is never forgotten. What seemed like a puzzle hours before became a clear picture of the new relationship possible with those who die.

WHAT HAPPENS WHEN A CHRISTIAN DIES?

This is a question asked of Paul by the early church in Corinth. They did not have hundreds of years of tradition and understanding the faith as we have experienced. When a Christian in the early church died, there were questions of exactly what was involved.

The Apostle Paul gives a beautiful picture of God's work at death. Remember, Paul was a tent maker by trade. He made tents from animal skins, many times working at this skill during his missionary journeys. In answer to the question from the church at Corinth, Paul replied:

> Now we know that if the earthly tent we live in is destroyed, we have a building from God, an eternal house in heaven, not built by human hands. Meanwhile we groan, longing to be clothed with our heavenly dwelling, because when we are clothed, we will not be found naked. For while we are in this tent, we groan and are burdened, because we do not wish to be unclothed but to be clothed with our heavenly dwelling, so that what is mortal may be swallowed up by life. Now it is God who has made us for this very purpose and has given us the Spirit as a deposit, guaranteeing what is to come.
>
> Therefore we are always confident and know that as long as we are at home in the body we are away from the Lord. We live by faith, not by sight. We are confident, I say, and would prefer to be away from the body and at home with the Lord. So we make it our goal to please him, whether we are at

home in the body or away from it. For we must all appear before the judgment seat of Christ, that each one may receive what is due him for the things done while in the body, whether good or bad.

II Corinthians 5:1–10

"I'M WITH YOU THROUGH THOSE NIGHTS"

In those darkened, endless hours
Of lingering nights of fear,
A voice softly whispers,
"Don't be afraid, I'm near."

"Though you feel alone
And you find Me hard to see,
I'm here and watching just the same
Most protectively."

"I know you feel abandoned
As you face this loss,
Even My Son felt deserted
As He hung upon the cross."

"In His deepest agony,
He felt separation, too,
From His own Father who had sent Him
In His mission to see through."

"If I can turn Good Friday into Easter
With all the suffering Jesus had,
Trust I'll bring good to you
From what now seems so bad."

Then in the shadowed darkness
Of the silence of the night,
The softly spoken message
Brought some hope in sight.

It gave courage to hold onto
In the midst of the unknown
To have heard the voice of God
When I felt so all alone.

I knew if His Son suffered
To accomplish what was willed,
God felt my suffering, too,
And would see my needs fulfilled.

©11/30/1998 D. Golden Boyd

PERSONAL NOTES

_____

_____

_____

_____

_____

_____

_____

_____

_____

_____

_____

_____

_____

_____

_____

_____

_____

_____

_____

_____

_____

_____

_____

_____

_____

_____

_____

_____

THE WORDS OF COMMITMENT

It was now about the sixth hour, and darkness came over the whole land until the ninth hour, for the sun stopped shining. And the curtain of the temple was torn in two. Jesus called out with a loud voice, "Father, into your hands I commit my spirit." When he had said this, he breathed his last.

Luke 23:44–46

These are the final words of Christ before His death on the cross. After His resurrection He spoke again to His disciples and followers. But these are His last words as the Savior of the world from Calvary's cross.

With these words, Christ was passing from God's earthly care to God's heavenly care. He was entrusting His soul, His Spirit, and His breath into the mighty hands of His heavenly Father.

> The psalmist, David, had prophesied these words.
>
> In you, O LORD, I have taken refuge; let me never be put to shame; deliver me in your righteousness. Turn your ear to me,
>
> come quickly to my rescue; be my rock of refuge, a strong fortress to save me. Since you are my rock and my fortress, for the sake of your name lead and guide me. Free me from the trap that is set for me, for you are my refuge. Into your hands I commit my spirit; redeem me, O LORD, the God of truth.
>
> Psalms 31:1–5

The committing of one's spirit into the hands of God is a holy time. This is an expression of complete and total trust, acknowledging our faith and reliance in His strength.

Stephen was a witness for Christ in the early church. Because of his boldness and faithfulness to

Christ, he was stoned to death. The Apostle Paul was an eyewitness to this stoning. Even though he was consenting to the death of Stephen, the experience had a profound impact upon his life.

> When they heard this, they were furious and gnashed their teeth at him. But Stephen, full of the Holy Spirit, looked up to heaven and saw the glory of God, and Jesus standing at the right hand of God. "Look," he said, "I see heaven open and the Son of Man standing at the right hand of God." At this they covered their ears and, yelling at the top of their voices, they all rushed at him, dragged him out of the city and began to stone him. Meanwhile, the witnesses laid their clothes at the feet of a young man named Saul. While they were stoning him, Stephen prayed, "Lord Jesus, receive my spirit." Then he fell on his knees and cried out, "Lord, do not hold this sin against them." When he had said this, he fell asleep.
>
> Acts 7:54–60

GIVING PERMISSION

We can only do so much; we can only go so far. Our strength can only sustain us for a certain period; then we are exhausted.

Christ was the Almighty, the miracle worker. He could have spoken the words, and angels would have appeared from heaven to intervene. All of His pain and suffering could have ended if He had only cried out to His Father. But, instead, He used His last breath to place His soul into the hands of a loving Father.

Giving permission is not giving up. Giving a loved one permission to place their spirit into God's hands is expressing the greatest love for them, and the greatest trust in God. As family members and caregivers, we need to release our loved one into the hands of God. We can do a wonderful job of providing for someone physically, but we are still limited. We can even meet the emotional needs of a loved one, but we are still limited. We can place the spiritual needs of our loved one into His hands, but we are still limited. However, God is not limited.

Our loved ones, the care-receivers, also have a responsibility to their families. Not only is it important for loved ones to hear everything is going to be okay, they also need to express that they are at peace with God and prepared for this time.

It is a very healthy thing for loved ones to give permission to one another. It may be expressed through words such as "It's okay, I'm going to be okay;" "You will never be forgotten, never;" "I will see you in heaven again very soon."

A COMMITMENT RITUAL

This is a very special, very holy time. It is a time for family members and caregivers to place the Spirit of their loved one into the hands of God. It is not giving up, but it is placing complete trust and confidence in God.

Seek to create the opportunity for a commitment ritual with your loved one. Invite all family members to participate, realizing there will be some who cannot do so. Gather around the loved one, hold hands, and recite this prayer of commitment:

Lord, we believe you to be the Ultimate Caregiver, so it is into your hands we commit the Spirit of our loved one. Wrap them with your love, your comfort, and your presence; fill us with your faith,

draw near to us with your comfort, sustain us
with the promises in your Word each day.

Amen

ARE YOU FACING TOWARD ME?

It was a devastating death in the rural community.
The young wife died suddenly, leaving behind her
husband and a son. There was a great outpouring of
sympathy for the family. The small church had an
overflow crowd at her funeral.

Following the service, family and friends gathered
in the home to offer comfort to the husband and son.
It was late when everyone left the home. The father
and young son found themselves alone in the home
for the first time.

As bedtime approached, the dad tucked his son
into bed, hugged him tightly, and said "I love you son.
I love you." As he left the room, he turned the light
off, and it grew very dark in that part of the house.

After the dad settled into his own bed, he reached
over and turned the lamp off. It was quiet and dark in
the house. In just a few minutes he heard the voice of
his son, "Daddy, can I come sleep with you?"

Realizing the difficult time they were both having,

he went to his son's room and carried him to his own room. After they settled into the bed, dad reached over and turned off the lamp again. It was so dark in the house, it was impossible to see even the form of the young boy in his arms.

In a few minutes the quietness was broken again with the voice of the boy, "Daddy, are you facing toward me?"

Dad said, "Yes, son, I'm facing toward you. Why are you asking?"

"Because it's real dark, and I'm afraid," said the young boy. "If I know you are facing toward me I think I can rest and go to sleep." In just a few short minutes, the dad could tell his son had fallen asleep in his arms.

Moved by the simple trust of his son, the father laid his head back upon his pillow and looked up to Heaven. "Father, are you facing toward me?" he asked. "It's real dark in my world right now, and I'm afraid. If I know you are facing toward me, I think I can rest and go to sleep."

This story illustrates the truth of God's presence. Even when you can't see Him or feel Him, He is there. As a caregiver or a care-receiver, there will be times of darkness and fear, but He is always facing toward you. We can lean upon the promises of the Ultimate Caregiver.

"Never will I leave you; never will I forsake you."

Hebrews 13:5

"SHOW ME CLEARLY"

God, You promise through the val-
leys when things get really bad,
You feel our hurt and wipe our tears
through times we feel so sad.

You said those times we stum-
ble and think we're on our own,
You'll pick us up and carry us and
make Your presence known.

You've said when burdens that we
carry seem too much to bear,
That you'll give strength we need
and take part of them to share.

You've assured when prayers we've
sent appear to not be heard,
You know us better than we know ourselves and answer every word.

You've reminded through confusion when we cannot understand,
That Your good can work through bad
and You have a mighty plan.

I try to keep in mind these things I
have in the past been taught,
But fail to trust in what You've said
and find the peace I ought.

Draw me in a little closer to make
Your will more clear,
And, please, forgive my human fail-
ings in remembering You are near.

Through all Your reassurance, I should
know how much You care,
But right now, I am so weak and
feel I have too much to bear.

Show me clearly You are with me
and help me try to cope,
And take my nagging doubts and fears
and replace them with some hope.

©01/05/1999 D. Golden Boyd

PERSONAL NOTES

_____

_____

_____

_____

_____

_____

_____

_____

_____

_____

EPILOGUE

In the midst of the weariness, uncertainty, and challenges for both the caregiver and care-receiver, there is a common thread. This thread is woven through all of the statements Christ made from the cross of Calvary. It blends into His statements so naturally, it takes careful consideration to recognize this necessary ingredient.

The necessary thread woven into the seven sayings of Christ on the cross? Trust!

Christ has provided the perfect model of trust. He provides a picture of placing faith in the heavenly Father during a time of trials. Consider the model He has established for us as the Ultimate Caregiver:

He trusted His heavenly Father to forgive those

who had beat Him, mocked Him, tortured Him, rejected Him, abandoned Him, and crucified Him.

He trusted His heavenly Father to provide salvation to the thief hanging next to Him, to receive Him into paradise immediately.

He trusted His heavenly Father to enable a disciple to provide care and comfort to Mary, the mother God had chosen for Him.

He trusted His heavenly Father to provide physical, emotional, and spiritual strength to Him as He thirsted during His time of suffering.

He trusted His heavenly Father to understand His expression of abandonment as He hung upon the cross.

He trusted His heavenly Father to receive the work He had completed, the mission He had accomplished on earth.

He trusted His heavenly Father to receive His Spirit as He died upon the cross, paying the price for the sins of man.

We are called upon to join the Son of God in this walk of trust, committing our entire faith into His hands.

And without faith it is impossible to please God, because anyone who comes to him must believe that he exists and that he rewards those who earnestly seek him.

Hebrews 11:6

Will you take this time to draw near to the Ultimate Caregiver? Jesus Christ loved us so much that He was willing to sacrifice His life so we might experience everlasting life.

Do not let your hearts be troubled. Trust in God; trust also in me. In my Father's house are many rooms; if it were not so, I would have told you. I am going there to prepare a place for you. And if I go and prepare a place for you, I will come back and take you to be with me that you also may be where I am. You know the way to the place where I am going.

Thomas said to him, "Lord, we don't know where you are going, so how can we know the way?"

Jesus answered, "I am the way and the truth and the life. No one comes to the Father except through me."

John 14:1–6

"GIFT OF DAYS"

No one knows the tomorrow
And life goes by so fast,
Days are to be seized
Before they are past.

Thoughts in the head
That tell us to do good,
Are chances we're given
To do as we should.

The health that we're given
May not always stay,
And our life on earth
Will end someday.

When love is felt for someone,
They should be told so,
Before they leave this earth
And perhaps never know.

Time cannot be wasted
And dwindled away,

There's opportunities to snatch
In each given day.

Life is to be lived
In the most meaningful ways,
In grateful thanks to God
For His gifts of our days.

©01/07/1999 D. Golden Boyd

PERSONAL NOTES

_____

_____

_____

_____

_____

_____

_____

_____

APPENDIX A

Normal Responses to Change

- "Numbness" to people and events around you, feeling out of place

- A feeling of tightness in the throat or heaviness in the chest

- A feeling of emptiness in the stomach and change in eating habits

- Feelings of restlessness and difficulty concentrating

- Feeling as though the change isn't real, as if it's a bad dream

- Wandering aimlessly and forgetting to finish projects

- Having a difficult time going to sleep, or wanting to sleep constantly

- Feelings of guilt or regret, thinking you could have done or said something that would have prevented the change from taking place

- Feelings of helplessness

- Feelings of being trapped in a situation, frustrated with everything

- Feelings of intense anger

- Blaming self, God, loved ones, and others

- Feelings of being cheated in life

- Feeling that life is not fair

- Overwhelmed with added responsibilities

- Fearful of the unknown future

- Feeling disregarded and even disrespected

- Feeling a need to protect others by not talking about the change

- Needing to talk to someone about the change and its impact on your life

- Mood changes over the slightest things, having some good days and some bad days, actually having good "moments" and bad "moments"

- Tears at unexpected times

APPENDIX B

The Caregiver Bill of Rights

As a caregiver, you have a right...

- To take care of yourself also
- To simplify your lifestyle
- To allow others to help you
- To take one day at a time
- To have a sense of humor
- To focus on the positive

- To participate in activities other than caregiving

- To walk out of the room and take a deep breath

- To tell family and friends how they can help you

- To maintain meaningful and supportive relationships

- To make time for yourself away from your caregiving role

- To make decisions based upon the needs of the patient and yourself

- To say no

- To accept your feelings without feeling guilty

- To forgive yourself for mistakes and outbursts

- To seek ways to renew yourself spiritually, physically, and emotionally

- To develop a support system of safe friends

- To grieve and to mourn, as a care-griever

APPENDIX C

Searching the Scriptures

- When you need peace ... John 14
- When you are anxious ... Psalm 121
- When you are discouraged ... Psalm 23
- When you feel deserted by friends ... I Corinthians 13
- When you are depressed ... Psalm 71
- When you are worried ... Psalm 46
- When you are facing a crisis ... Isaiah 55

- When you are holding a grudge ... Ephesians 4
- When you have weak faith ... Psalm 126
- When you think God is distant ... Psalm 25
- When you are lonely ... John 11
- When you are afraid ... II Timothy 1:7
- When you are doubting ... Hebrews 11:1–6
- When you are grieving ... II Corinthians 1:3–5
- When you need guidance ... Proverbs 3:5–6
- When you are overcome ... Romans 8:31–39
- When you are sorrowful ... Psalm 51
- When you are weary ... Psalm 90
- When you need courage ... Ephesians 6:10–18
- When you need comfort ... Romans 8:26–28

APPENDIX D

Making a Checklist

Perhaps the following checklist will help you find a beginning place to organize your life at this difficult and confusing time.

- Living will, power of attorney

- Trusts, most up to date will, contact information for your lawyer

- Military discharge papers

- Funeral arrangements

- Legal paperwork on real estate, mortgages, etc.

- Social Security and Medicare information

- Social Security card

- Insurance policies (life, health, home, and car)

- Bank name and account numbers

- Physician names and contact numbers

- Medications, prescriptions, pharmacy contact information

- Investments and retirement information

- Deeds to property

- Divorce decree, child custody paperwork

- Birth certificates

- Income tax returns

- Sources of income and assets, investments, etc.

- Credit and debit card names and contact numbers

Put all of your important documents in one place and inform a trusted family member or friend of that location.

APPENDIX E

Capturing Family Treasures

Do you know if your grandfather had a pet? What type of house did your mother live in as a child? Who influenced your father's life? The only way you could know the answers to these questions would be if they had been recorded in some manner. Unfortunately, personal information, stories, and influences are lost unless they are shared and recorded.

The following guide can provide a starting point to record life reflections of a loved one. Set aside time, perhaps in several sessions, to talk with your loved one. Record the answers in a journal, gaining as much insight as possible into their life. Look for additional questions and subjects that would provide valuable insight. Remember, you are capturing a family treasure.

What is your favorite childhood memory?

What kind of pet did you have as a child?

What was the house like you remember most as a child?

Who was your first best friend as you grew up?

What was the most trouble you ever got into?

When you needed help, who could you count on?

What was the best trip or vacation you ever took?

When did you first meet your spouse?

What is your most prized possession?

What is your favorite movie?

What is the most amazing technological advance you have seen?

Who had the greatest spiritual impact on your life?

What has been your greatest heartache in life?

What has been your greatest fear in life?

Name five people who had a large impact upon your life.

Name five very important decisions you have made in your life.

Name five lessons life has taught you.

As you visit with your loved one to capture this information, please be aware that some of these responses might elicit emotions from them. This could be a time of laughter, even a time of tears. As the answers to these questions are being recorded, they are becoming family treasures. These answers cannot be purchased in any store, and they would be lost if they are not captured by someone who cares.

APPENDIX F

The Healing Heart

"Can you make a sculpture from a photograph?" I turned to face the person who spoke these words and looked into the faces of a three-generation family. As we spoke, one of the women opened an envelope and began spreading the photos of a young boy across the table in front of me.

"Could you take some photos from the side so I can have a profile view?" I asked. The woman quickly uttered a statement that had probably been rehearsed a hundred times in her mind. "This is our three-and-a-half-year-old grandson, Malachi. He drowned two weeks ago in our backyard." Tears streamed down her face as she said, "We were in your gallery last month, and Malachi was with us. After his funeral my husband said we should come see if you could sculpt a bust of Malachi."

She shared that they were having a very difficult time; they loved Malachi so very deeply. I heard how their faith in God was supporting them, how they were finding strength in His presence each day, and in one another. There had been many heartaches in their lives, but nothing had broken their hearts like the death of Malachi.

During the process of sculpting the bust of Malachi, the Lord inspired me to sculpt The Healing Heart.

> He heals the brokenhearted and binds up their wounds.
>
> Psalm 147:3

The Healing Heart has scars upon it to represent past losses that have healed. This family had suffered many other losses over the years. The Healing Heart has a break to symbolize a tragic event that breaks the heart. Malachi's death was the event that broke the hearts in this family. The Healing Heart has a bandage placed over the break to represent the healing power and presence of God. Bandages do not heal. They only hold you together while the Lord is bringing about the healing.

The Healing Heart sculpture symbolizes the heart of the caregiver and the care-receiver. There have been losses in the past, your hearts are broken due to changes being experienced, but something is holding everything together each day. Caregivers and care-receivers grow weary, but they are held together because of the needs that bond them.

Often the bandage holding everyone together is the presence and precious support of friends and family members. This bandage can also represent your faith in Jesus Christ, holding your life together while He is healing relationships as the Ultimate Caregiver.

Bob Willis, Sculptor

For more information on purchasing The Healing Heart sculpture by Bob Willis,

log onto:
www.Godhealshearts.com

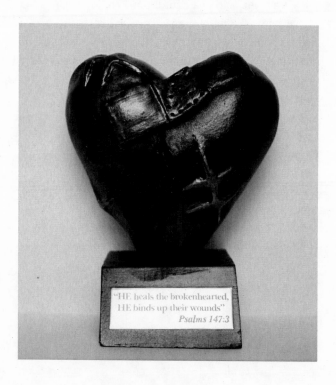

"FORCED TO TRUST"

When I begin to doubt
And fear what's left to face,
I have to remind myself
God's brought me to this place.

He's managed to be with me
And seen me through this far,
And I need to trust He'll be there
In the next obstacles there are.

Otherwise, I'd give up
And collapse in my despair,
Because I know that on my own,
It'd be too much to bear.

It's almost like the spot I'm in
Forces faith unknown before,
Because there is no other choice
To get through what is in store.

Perhaps that's the biggest lesson
In this trial I'm going through,

That it all rests in His hands
No matter what I try to do.

And that when I'm down the lowest,
I must believe that He is there,
'Cause I can't handle it myself
And have to leave it in His care.

©1/4/99 D. Golden Boyd

CONTACT
INFORMATION

Bob Willis, author of The Ultimate Caregiver, is also an accomplished sculptor. His unique presentation of The Ultimate Caregiver has a lasting impact upon caregivers, care-receivers, and professionals as he sculpts a bust of Christ or The Healing Heart sculpture while sharing valuable insight into the caregiving experience.

Contact Bob to arrange for this unique presentation of The Ultimate Caregiver to your group or conference:

Bob Willis
P.O. Box 1286
Edmond, OK 73083–1286
(405) 330–4910

The Healing Heart sculpture is also a creation of Bob Willis. The story behind the development of The Healing Heart is provided in Appendix F. This sculpture of a broken heart with a bandage to symbolize support provides a perfect sympathy gift for anyone following a loss or life crisis. It serves as a testimony to the comforting power and presence of the Lord during a time of heartache.

For more information on purchasing The Healing Heart sculpture, log onto:

www.Godhealshearts.com

BIOGRAPHY

Bob Willis has been an ordained Southern Baptist minister since 1979, serving churches in Kentucky, Tennessee, and Oklahoma. Since 1995 he has served as Bereavement Coordinator for Hospice of Oklahoma County in Oklahoma City. He provides grief support and counseling for hospice patients and family members, while facilitating grief support groups for the community. Bob is a frequent speaker on grief, loss, and caregiving issues on the state, regional, and national levels.

Bob and his wife, Lynn, live in Edmond, Oklahoma. They are the parents of a son, Eric, and a daughter, Kristi. They are also proud grandparents of seven grandsons and one granddaughter.

Bob and Lynn present The Gospel in Clay in churches throughout the Midwest. While Bob uses clay to sculpt a bust of Christ with a crown of thorns, Lynn sings of His sacrifice on the cross. This unique blend of sculpture, music, testimony, and Scriptures offers a memorable worship experience. It presents a challenge to be molded into the image of the Ultimate Caregiver, Jesus Christ.

To arrange for Bob and Lynn to minister through The Gospel in Clay in your church or retreat setting, please contact them at:

(405) 330–4910
Email: rwillis14@cox.net

ENDNOTES

1   Carter, Rosalyn with Susan K. Golant. Helping Yourself Help Others: A Book for Caregivers. New York: Times Books, 1994.

2   "Marianne Williamson," ThinkExist.com Quotations, 1999–2006.

    <http://www.thinkexist.com/quotes>

3   Cowper, William. "There Is a Fountain Filled with Blood." Conyer's Collections of Psalms and Hymns; 1772.

4   "Billy Graham," <http://brainyquote.com> January 2008.

5   "Corrie Ten Boom," <http://brainyquote.com> January
     2008.

6   Moncur, Michael. "Payne Stewart," QuotationsPage.com.
     1994–2008.

     <http://quotationspage.com>

7   "Ralph Waldo Emerson," ThinkExist.com Quotations,
     1999–2006.

     <http://www.thinkexist.com/quotes>